GUEST BOOK TO CELEBRATE :

_____

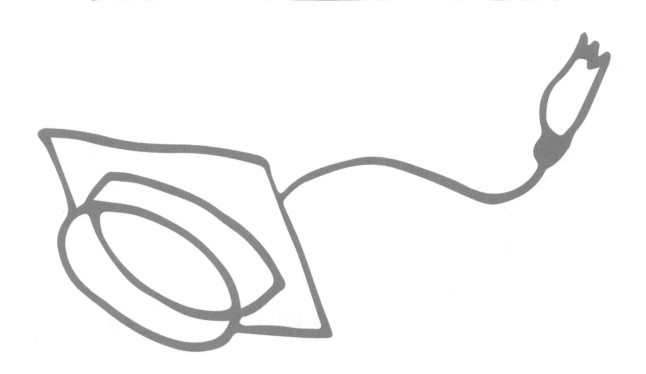

ADVICE AND WISHES FOR THE GRADUATE

Be prepared to..

....

Always keep...

....

Focus on...

never...

Always remember...

....

Be open to...

Surround yourself with..

I wish you..

....

(one last thing)...

BEST WISHES ∘∘∘∘∘∘∘∘∘∘∘∘∘∘∘∘∘∘∘∘∘∘∘∘∘∘∘∘∘∘∘∘∘∘∘

ADVICE AND WISHES FOR THE GRADUATE

Be prepared to...

....

Always keep...

....

Focus on...

never..

Always remember...

....

Be open to..

Surround yourself with...

I wish you...

....

(one last thing)..

BEST WISHES ∘∘∘∘∘∘∘∘∘∘∘∘∘∘∘∘∘∘∘∘∘∘∘∘∘∘∘∘∘∘∘∘∘∘∘∘∘

ADVICE AND WISHES FOR THE GRADUATE

Be prepared to..
....

Always keep...
....

Focus on...
never...

Always remember..
....

Be open to...
Surround yourself with...
I wish you...
....
(one last thing)...

BEST WISHES ○○○○○○○○○○○○○○○○○○○○○○○○○○○○○○○○○○○○○○

ADVICE AND WISHES FOR THE GRADUATE

Be prepared to...

....

Always keep...

....

Focus on...

never...

Always remember...

....

Be open to...

Surround yourself with...

I wish you...

....

(one last thing)...

BEST WISHES ooooooooooooooooooooooooooooooooooooooo

ADVICE AND WISHES FOR THE GRADUATE

Be prepared to...
....

Always keep...
....

Focus on..
never...

Always remember..
....

Be open to..
Surround yourself with...
I wish you...
....

(one last thing)...

BEST WISHES °°

ADVICE AND WISHES FOR THE GRADUATE

Be prepared to...

....

Always keep...

....

Focus on..

never...

Always remember...

....

Be open to...

Surround yourself with...

I wish you...

....

(one last thing)..

BEST WISHES °°°

ADVICE AND WISHES FOR THE GRADUATE

Be prepared to..

....

Always keep..

....

Focus on..

never..

Always remember..

....

Be open to..

Surround yourself with..

I wish you..

....

(one last thing)..

BEST WISHES ○○○○○○○○○○○○○○○○○○○○○○○○○○○○○○○○○○○○○○○

ADVICE AND WISHES FOR THE GRADUATE

Be prepared to..
....

Always keep..
....

Focus on...
never...

Always remember...
....

Be open to...

Surround yourself with..

I wish you...
....

(one last thing)..

BEST WISHES ∘∘∘∘∘∘∘∘∘∘∘∘∘∘∘∘∘∘∘∘∘∘∘∘∘∘∘∘∘∘∘∘∘∘

ADVICE AND WISHES FOR THE GRADUATE

Be prepared to..

....

Always keep..

....

Focus on..

never..

Always remember..

....

Be open to..

Surround yourself with..

I wish you..

....

(one last thing)..

BEST WISHES ∘∘∘∘∘∘∘∘∘∘∘∘∘∘∘∘∘∘∘∘∘∘∘∘∘∘∘∘∘∘∘∘∘∘∘∘∘∘

ADVICE AND WISHES FOR THE GRADUATE

Be prepared to..

....

Always keep..

....

Focus on..

never...

Always remember...

....

Be open to..

Surround yourself with...

I wish you...

....

(one last thing)..

BEST WISHES ∘∘∘∘∘∘∘∘∘∘∘∘∘∘∘∘∘∘∘∘∘∘∘∘∘∘∘∘∘∘∘∘∘

ADVICE AND WISHES FOR THE GRADUATE

Be prepared to..

....

Always keep..

....

Focus on..

never...

Always remember...

....

Be open to...

Surround yourself with...

I wish you..

....

(one last thing)..

BEST WISHES ....

ADVICE AND WISHES FOR THE GRADUATE

Be prepared to...

....

Always keep..

....

Focus on..

never...

Always remember..

....

Be open to...

Surround yourself with..

I wish you...

....

(one last thing)..

BEST WISHES ○○

ADVICE AND WISHES FOR THE GRADUATE

Be prepared to...

....

Always keep...

....

Focus on...

never..

Always remember...

....

Be open to...

Surround yourself with..

I wish you...

....

(one last thing)...

BEST WISHES ooooooooooooooooooooooooooooooooooooooooo

ADVICE AND WISHES FOR THE GRADUATE

Be prepared to..

....

Always keep...

....

Focus on..

never...

Always remember..

....

Be open to..

Surround yourself with...

I wish you..

....

(one last thing)..

BEST WISHES ∘∘∘

ADVICE AND WISHES FOR THE GRADUATE

Be prepared to...

....

Always keep...

....

Focus on..

never...

Always remember...

....

Be open to...

Surround yourself with..

I wish you..

....

(one last thing)..

BEST WISHES °°

ADVICE AND WISHES FOR THE GRADUATE

Be prepared to...

....

Always keep..

....

Focus on...

never...

Always remember..

....

Be open to..

Surround yourself with...

I wish you...

....

(one last thing)...

BEST WISHES ....

ADVICE AND WISHES FOR THE GRADUATE

Be prepared to..
....

Always keep..
....

Focus on..
never..
Always remember...
....

Be open to..
Surround yourself with..
I wish you...
....

(one last thing)..

BEST WISHES ∘∘∘∘∘∘∘∘∘∘∘∘∘∘∘∘∘∘∘∘∘∘∘∘∘∘∘∘∘∘∘∘∘∘

ADVICE AND WISHES FOR THE GRADUATE

Be prepared to..
....

Always keep...
....

Focus on..
never...

Always remember...
....

Be open to..

Surround yourself with..

I wish you..
....

(one last thing)..

BEST WISHES ∘∘

ADVICE AND WISHES FOR THE GRADUATE

Be prepared to...

....

Always keep..

....

Focus on...

never..

Always remember..

....

Be open to..

Surround yourself with..

I wish you...

....

(one last thing)..

BEST WISHES ○○○○○○○○○○○○○○○○○○○○○○○○○○○○○○○○○○

ADVICE AND WISHES FOR THE GRADUATE

Be prepared to..

....

Always keep...

....

Focus on..

never...

Always remember...

....

Be open to...

Surround yourself with..

I wish you..

....

(one last thing)..

BEST WISHES °°°°°°°°°°°°°°°°°°°°°°°°°°°°°°°°°°°

ADVICE AND WISHES FOR THE GRADUATE

Be prepared to..
....
Always keep..
....
Focus on...
never..
Always remember..
....
Be open to...
Surround yourself with...
I wish you...
....
(one last thing)...

BEST WISHES ....

ADVICE AND WISHES FOR THE GRADUATE

Be prepared to...
....

Always keep...
....

Focus on...

never...

Always remember...
....

Be open to...

Surround yourself with...

I wish you...
....

(one last thing)...

BEST WISHES ∘∘∘∘∘∘∘∘∘∘∘∘∘∘∘∘∘∘∘∘∘∘∘∘∘∘∘∘∘∘∘∘∘∘

ADVICE AND WISHES FOR THE GRADUATE

Be prepared to..

....

Always keep..

....

Focus on..

never..

Always remember..

....

Be open to..

Surround yourself with..

I wish you..

....

(one last thing)..

BEST WISHES ○○○○○○○○○○○○○○○○○○○○○○○○○○○○○○○○○○

ADVICE AND WISHES FOR THE GRADUATE

Be prepared to..
....

Always keep..
....

Focus on..
never..
Always remember..
....

Be open to..
Surround yourself with..
I wish you..
....
(one last thing)..

BEST WISHES ....

ADVICE AND WISHES FOR THE GRADUATE

Be prepared to..

....

Always keep...

....

Focus on..

never..

Always remember..

....

Be open to...

Surround yourself with...

I wish you...

....

(one last thing)..

BEST WISHES ○○○○○○○○○○○○○○○○○○○○○○○○○○○○○○○○○○○○○

ADVICE AND WISHES FOR THE GRADUATE

Be prepared to...

....

Always keep...

....

Focus on..

never..

Always remember...

....

Be open to...

Surround yourself with...

I wish you..

....

(one last thing)..

BEST WISHES ∘∘∘∘∘∘∘∘∘∘∘∘∘∘∘∘∘∘∘∘∘∘∘∘∘∘∘∘∘∘∘∘∘∘∘∘∘∘∘

ADVICE AND WISHES FOR THE GRADUATE

Be prepared to...

....

Always keep...

....

Focus on...

never..

Always remember...

....

Be open to..

Surround yourself with...

I wish you...

....

(one last thing)...

BEST WISHES ○○○○○○○○○○○○○○○○○○○○○○○○○○○○○○○○○○○○○○

ADVICE AND WISHES FOR THE GRADUATE

Be prepared to..

....

Always keep..

....

Focus on...

never..

Always remember..

....

Be open to..

Surround yourself with..

I wish you...

....

(one last thing)...

BEST WISHES ○○○○○○○○○○○○○○○○○○○○○○○○○○○○○○○○○○

ADVICE AND WISHES FOR THE GRADUATE

Be prepared to..
....

Always keep..
....

Focus on..

never..

Always remember..
....

Be open to..

Surround yourself with..

I wish you..
....

(one last thing)..

BEST WISHES ∘∘∘∘∘∘∘∘∘∘∘∘∘∘∘∘∘∘∘∘∘∘∘∘∘∘∘∘∘

ADVICE AND WISHES FOR THE GRADUATE

Be prepared to..

....

Always keep..

....

Focus on...

never...

Always remember...

....

Be open to..

Surround yourself with...

I wish you...

....

(one last thing)...

BEST WISHES ○○○○○○○○○○○○○○○○○○○○○○○○○○○○○○○○○○

ADVICE AND WISHES FOR THE GRADUATE

Be prepared to...

....

Always keep...

....

Focus on..

never...

Always remember...

....

Be open to...

Surround yourself with..

I wish you..

....

(one last thing)..

BEST WISHES ....

ADVICE AND WISHES FOR THE GRADUATE

Be prepared to...
....

Always keep...
....

Focus on..

never...

Always remember...
....

Be open to..

Surround yourself with..

I wish you..
....

(one last thing)..

BEST WISHES ooooooooooooooooooooooooooooooooooo

ADVICE AND WISHES FOR THE GRADUATE

Be prepared to...

....

Always keep...

....

Focus on...

never...

Always remember...

....

Be open to...

Surround yourself with...

I wish you...

....

(one last thing)...

BEST WISHES ○○○○○○○○○○○○○○○○○○○○○○○○○○○○○○○

ADVICE AND WISHES FOR THE GRADUATE

Be prepared to..

....

Always keep..

....

Focus on...

never...

Always remember..

....

Be open to...

Surround yourself with...

I wish you...

....

(one last thing)...

BEST WISHES ....

ADVICE AND WISHES FOR THE GRADUATE

Be prepared to...

....

Always keep..

....

Focus on...

never...

Always remember...

....

Be open to..

Surround yourself with...

I wish you...

....

(one last thing)..

BEST WISHES ....

ADVICE AND WISHES FOR THE GRADUATE

Be prepared to..

....

Always keep..

....

Focus on..

never..

Always remember..

....

Be open to..

Surround yourself with..

I wish you..

....

(one last thing)..

BEST WISHES ....

ADVICE AND WISHES FOR THE GRADUATE

Be prepared to..
....

Always keep...
....

Focus on...
never..

Always remember...
....

Be open to..

Surround yourself with..

I wish you...
....

(one last thing)..

BEST WISHES ....

ADVICE AND WISHES FOR THE GRADUATE

Be prepared to..

....

Always keep...

....

Focus on..

never..

Always remember..

....

Be open to...

Surround yourself with...

I wish you..

....

(one last thing)...

BEST WISHES °°

ADVICE AND WISHES FOR THE GRADUATE

Be prepared to..
....

Always keep...
....

Focus on...
never...
Always remember...
....

Be open to..
Surround yourself with...
I wish you...
....
(one last thing)..

BEST WISHES ∘∘∘∘∘∘∘∘∘∘∘∘∘∘∘∘∘∘∘∘∘∘∘∘∘∘∘∘∘∘∘∘∘∘∘

ADVICE AND WISHES FOR THE GRADUATE

Be prepared to...

....

Always keep..

....

Focus on...

never...

Always remember..

....

Be open to..

Surround yourself with...

I wish you..

....

(one last thing)...

BEST WISHES ∘∘∘∘∘∘∘∘∘∘∘∘∘∘∘∘∘∘∘∘∘∘∘∘∘∘∘∘∘∘∘∘∘∘∘∘∘

ADVICE AND WISHES FOR THE GRADUATE

Be prepared to...
....

Always keep...
....

Focus on...
never...
Always remember...
....

Be open to...
Surround yourself with...
I wish you...
....

(one last thing)...

BEST WISHES ....

ADVICE AND WISHES FOR THE GRADUATE

Be prepared to..

....

Always keep..

....

Focus on..

never...

Always remember...

....

Be open to..

Surround yourself with..

I wish you..

....

(one last thing)..

BEST WISHES ∘∘∘∘∘∘∘∘∘∘∘∘∘∘∘∘∘∘∘∘∘∘∘∘∘∘∘∘∘∘∘

ADVICE AND WISHES FOR THE GRADUATE

Be prepared to..

....

Always keep..

....

Focus on...

never...

Always remember..

....

Be open to..

Surround yourself with...

I wish you...

....

(one last thing)..

BEST WISHES ....

ADVICE AND WISHES FOR THE GRADUATE

Be prepared to...
....

Always keep..
....

Focus on..
never...

Always remember...
....

Be open to...

Surround yourself with..

I wish you..
....

(one last thing)...

BEST WISHES ∘∘∘∘∘∘∘∘∘∘∘∘∘∘∘∘∘∘∘∘∘∘∘∘∘∘∘∘∘∘∘∘

ADVICE AND WISHES FOR THE GRADUATE

Be prepared to...
....

Always keep...
....

Focus on..

never...

Always remember...
....

Be open to..

Surround yourself with...

I wish you..
....

(one last thing)...

BEST WISHES ○○○○○○○○○○○○○○○○○○○○○○○○○○○○○○○○○○○

ADVICE AND WISHES FOR THE GRADUATE

Be prepared to...

....

Always keep..

....

Focus on..

never..

Always remember...

....

Be open to..

Surround yourself with...

I wish you..

....

(one last thing)..

BEST WISHES ∘∘∘∘∘∘∘∘∘∘∘∘∘∘∘∘∘∘∘∘∘∘∘∘∘∘∘∘∘∘∘∘∘∘∘∘∘

ADVICE AND WISHES FOR THE GRADUATE

Be prepared to...
....

Always keep..
....

Focus on..

never..

Always remember..
....

Be open to...

Surround yourself with..

I wish you..
....

(one last thing)..

BEST WISHES ∘∘∘∘∘∘∘∘∘∘∘∘∘∘∘∘∘∘∘∘∘∘∘∘∘∘∘∘∘∘∘∘∘

ADVICE AND WISHES FOR THE GRADUATE

Be prepared to..
....

Always keep..
....

Focus on..

never..

Always remember..
....

Be open to..

Surround yourself with..

I wish you..
....

(one last thing)..

BEST WISHES ∘∘∘∘∘∘∘∘∘∘∘∘∘∘∘∘∘∘∘∘∘∘∘∘∘∘∘∘∘∘∘∘∘∘∘

ADVICE AND WISHES FOR THE GRADUATE

Be prepared to..

....

Always keep...

....

Focus on...

never...

Always remember...

....

Be open to..

Surround yourself with..

I wish you...

....

(one last thing)..

BEST WISHES ∘∘∘∘∘∘∘∘∘∘∘∘∘∘∘∘∘∘∘∘∘∘∘∘∘∘∘∘∘∘∘∘∘∘∘∘

ADVICE AND WISHES FOR THE GRADUATE

Be prepared to..

....

Always keep..

....

Focus on...

never..

Always remember...

....

Be open to...

Surround yourself with...

I wish you...

....

(one last thing)...

BEST WISHES ∘∘∘∘∘∘∘∘∘∘∘∘∘∘∘∘∘∘∘∘∘∘∘∘∘∘∘∘∘∘∘∘∘

ADVICE AND WISHES FOR THE GRADUATE

Be prepared to..
....

Always keep..
....

Focus on..

never...

Always remember..
....

Be open to..

Surround yourself with...

I wish you...
....

(one last thing)..

BEST WISHES ∘∘

ADVICE AND WISHES FOR THE GRADUATE

Be prepared to...
....

Always keep...
....

Focus on...
never..
Always remember...
....

Be open to..
Surround yourself with...
I wish you..
....
(one last thing)..

BEST WISHES ∘∘∘∘∘∘∘∘∘∘∘∘∘∘∘∘∘∘∘∘∘∘∘∘∘∘∘∘∘∘∘∘∘∘∘∘∘∘

ADVICE AND WISHES FOR THE GRADUATE

Be prepared to..
....

Always keep..

....

Focus on...
never...
Always remember...
....

Be open to..
Surround yourself with...
I wish you..
....
(one last thing)...

BEST WISHES ....

ADVICE AND WISHES FOR THE GRADUATE

Be prepared to...

....

Always keep...

....

Focus on...

never...

Always remember...

....

Be open to...

Surround yourself with...

I wish you...

....

(one last thing)...

BEST WISHES ∘∘∘∘∘∘∘∘∘∘∘∘∘∘∘∘∘∘∘∘∘∘∘∘∘∘∘∘∘∘∘∘∘∘∘∘∘

ADVICE AND WISHES FOR THE GRADUATE

Be prepared to...
....

Always keep..
....

Focus on..

never...

Always remember..
....

Be open to..

Surround yourself with..

I wish you..
....

(one last thing)...

BEST WISHES ∘∘∘∘∘∘∘∘∘∘∘∘∘∘∘∘∘∘∘∘∘∘∘∘∘∘∘∘∘∘∘∘∘∘∘∘

ADVICE AND WISHES FOR THE GRADUATE

Be prepared to..

....

Always keep...

....

Focus on..

never...

Always remember..

....

Be open to...

Surround yourself with...

I wish you...

....

(ONE LAST THING)..

BEST WISHES ∘∘

ADVICE AND WISHES FOR THE GRADUATE

Be prepared to...

....

Always keep...

....

Focus on...

never...

Always remember...

....

Be open to...

Surround yourself with...

I wish you...

....

(one last thing)...

BEST WISHES ∘∘∘∘∘∘∘∘∘∘∘∘∘∘∘∘∘∘∘∘∘∘∘∘∘∘∘∘∘∘∘∘∘∘∘∘

ADVICE AND WISHES FOR THE GRADUATE

Be prepared to..

....

Always keep..

....

Focus on..

never..

Always remember..

....

Be open to..

Surround yourself with...

I wish you..

....

(one last thing)..

BEST WISHES ∘∘∘∘∘∘∘∘∘∘∘∘∘∘∘∘∘∘∘∘∘∘∘∘∘∘∘∘∘∘∘

ADVICE AND WISHES FOR THE GRADUATE

Be prepared to...

....

Always keep..

....

Focus on..

never..

Always remember..

....

Be open to...

Surround yourself with...

I wish you..

....

(one last thing)...

BEST WISHES ∘∘

ADVICE AND WISHES FOR THE GRADUATE

Be prepared to..

....

Always keep..

....

Focus on...

never..

Always remember...

....

Be open to..

Surround yourself with..

I wish you...

....

(one last thing)..

BEST WISHES ○○○○○○○○○○○○○○○○○○○○○○○○○○○○○○○○○○

ADVICE AND WISHES FOR THE GRADUATE

Be prepared to..

....

Always keep...

....

Focus on...

never..

Always remember..

....

Be open to..

Surround yourself with...

I wish you...

....

(one last thing)..

BEST WISHES ○○○○○○○○○○○○○○○○○○○○○○○○○○○○○○○○○○○○

ADVICE AND WISHES FOR THE GRADUATE

Be prepared to...

....

Always keep...

....

Focus on...

never...

Always remember...

....

Be open to...

Surround yourself with...

I wish you...

....

(one last thing)...

BEST WISHES ....

ADVICE AND WISHES FOR THE GRADUATE

Be prepared to..

....

Always keep..

....

Focus on...

never..

Always remember..

....

Be open to..

Surround yourself with...

I wish you..

....

(one last thing)...

BEST WISHES ○○

ADVICE AND WISHES FOR THE GRADUATE

Be prepared to...
....

Always keep...
....

Focus on..

never..

Always remember...
....

Be open to..

Surround yourself with..

I wish you..
....

(one last thing)..

BEST WISHES ∘∘∘∘∘∘∘∘∘∘∘∘∘∘∘∘∘∘∘∘∘∘∘∘∘∘∘∘∘∘∘∘∘∘∘∘∘∘

ADVICE AND WISHES FOR THE GRADUATE

Be prepared to...

....

Always keep...

....

Focus on...

never...

Always remember...

....

Be open to...

Surround yourself with...

I wish you...

....

(one last thing)...

BEST WISHES ....

ADVICE AND WISHES FOR THE GRADUATE

Be prepared to..

....

Always keep...

....

Focus on..

never..

Always remember..

....

Be open to..

Surround yourself with...

I wish you...

....

(one last thing)..

BEST WISHES ∘∘∘∘∘∘∘∘∘∘∘∘∘∘∘∘∘∘∘∘∘∘∘∘∘∘∘∘∘∘∘∘∘∘∘

ADVICE AND WISHES FOR THE GRADUATE

Be prepared to...
....

Always keep...
....

Focus on..

never...

Always remember...
....

Be open to...

Surround yourself with..

I wish you...
....

(one last thing)..

BEST WISHES ∘∘∘∘∘∘∘∘∘∘∘∘∘∘∘∘∘∘∘∘∘∘∘∘∘∘∘∘∘∘∘∘∘∘∘∘

ADVICE AND WISHES FOR THE GRADUATE

Be prepared to...

....

Always keep...

....

Focus on...

never...

Always remember...

....

Be open to...

Surround yourself with...

I wish you...

....

(one last thing)...

BEST WISHES ooooooooooooooooooooooooooooooooooo

ADVICE AND WISHES FOR THE GRADUATE

Be prepared to...
....

Always keep...

....

Focus on...

never...

Always remember...

....

Be open to...

Surround yourself with...

I wish you...

....

(one last thing)...

BEST WISHES ....

ADVICE AND WISHES FOR THE GRADUATE

Be prepared to...

....

Always keep...

....

Focus on...

never...

Always remember...

....

Be open to...

Surround yourself with...

I wish you...

....

(one last thing)...

BEST WISHES ∘∘∘∘∘∘∘∘∘∘∘∘∘∘∘∘∘∘∘∘∘∘∘∘∘∘∘∘∘∘∘∘∘∘∘∘

ADVICE AND WISHES FOR THE GRADUATE

Be prepared to...
....

Always keep..
....

Focus on..
never..
Always remember..
....

Be open to..
Surround yourself with...
I wish you...
....
(one last thing)...

BEST WISHES ....

ADVICE AND WISHES FOR THE GRADUATE

Be prepared to..

....

Always keep..

....

Focus on..

never..

Always remember..

....

Be open to..

Surround yourself with..

I wish you..

....

(one last thing)..

BEST WISHES oooooooooooooooooooooooooooooooooooooo

ADVICE AND WISHES FOR THE GRADUATE

Be prepared to..

....

Always keep..

....

Focus on..

never..

Always remember..

....

Be open to..

Surround yourself with..

I wish you..

....

(one last thing)..

BEST WISHES ∘∘∘∘∘∘∘∘∘∘∘∘∘∘∘∘∘∘∘∘∘∘∘∘∘∘∘∘∘∘∘∘∘∘

ADVICE AND WISHES FOR THE GRADUATE

Be prepared to..

....

Always keep..

....

Focus on...

never...

Always remember..

....

Be open to...

Surround yourself with..

I wish you...

....

(one last thing)..

BEST WISHES ∘∘∘∘∘∘∘∘∘∘∘∘∘∘∘∘∘∘∘∘∘∘∘∘∘∘∘∘∘∘∘∘∘∘∘∘∘

ADVICE AND WISHES FOR THE GRADUATE

Be prepared to...

....

Always keep...

....

Focus on...

never...

Always remember...

....

Be open to...

Surround yourself with...

I wish you..

....

(one last thing)..

BEST WISHES ∘∘∘∘∘∘∘∘∘∘∘∘∘∘∘∘∘∘∘∘∘∘∘∘∘∘∘∘∘∘∘∘∘∘∘

ADVICE AND WISHES FOR THE GRADUATE

Be prepared to..

....

Always keep..

....

Focus on..

never..

Always remember..

....

Be open to..

Surround yourself with..

I wish you..

....

(one last thing)..

BEST WISHES °°°°°°°°°°°°°°°°°°°°°°°°°°°°°°°°°°°°°°

ADVICE AND WISHES FOR THE GRADUATE

Be prepared to..

....

Always keep...

....

Focus on...

never...

Always remember..

....

Be open to..

Surround yourself with...

I wish you...

....

(one last thing)..

BEST WISHES °°°°°°°°°°°°°°°°°°°°°°°°°°°°°°°°°°°°°°

ADVICE AND WISHES FOR THE GRADUATE

Be prepared to..

....

Always keep..

....

Focus on..

never..

Always remember..

....

Be open to..

Surround yourself with..

I wish you..

....

(one last thing)..

BEST WISHES ○○○○○○○○○○○○○○○○○○○○○○○○○○○○○○○○○○

ADVICE AND WISHES FOR THE GRADUATE

Be prepared to...

....

Always keep..

....

Focus on..

never..

Always remember..

....

Be open to..

Surround yourself with...

I wish you...

....

(one last thing)...

BEST WISHES ....

ADVICE AND WISHES FOR THE GRADUATE

Be prepared to..
....

Always keep...
....

Focus on..
never...

Always remember..
....

Be open to...

Surround yourself with..

I wish you..
....

(one last thing)..

BEST WISHES ∘∘∘∘∘∘∘∘∘∘∘∘∘∘∘∘∘∘∘∘∘∘∘∘∘∘∘∘∘∘∘∘∘∘∘

ADVICE AND WISHES FOR THE GRADUATE

Be prepared to...

....

Always keep...

....

Focus on...

never...

Always remember...

....

Be open to...

Surround yourself with...

I wish you...

....

(one last thing)...

BEST WISHES ○○○○○○○○○○○○○○○○○○○○○○○○○○○○○○○○○○

ADVICE AND WISHES FOR THE GRADUATE

Be prepared to..

....

Always keep..

....

Focus on...

never..

Always remember...

....

Be open to...

Surround yourself with...

I wish you...

....

(one last thing)...

BEST WISHES ∘∘∘

ADVICE AND WISHES FOR THE GRADUATE

Be prepared to...

....

Always keep...

....

Focus on..

never..

Always remember..

....

Be open to..

Surround yourself with..

I wish you..

....

(one last thing)..

BEST WISHES °°°

ADVICE AND WISHES FOR THE GRADUATE

Be prepared to...

....

Always keep..

....

Focus on...

never..

Always remember...

....

Be open to..

Surround yourself with..

I wish you..

....

(one last thing)..

BEST WISHES ∘∘∘∘∘∘∘∘∘∘∘∘∘∘∘∘∘∘∘∘∘∘∘∘∘∘∘∘∘∘∘∘∘∘∘∘∘∘∘

ADVICE AND WISHES FOR THE GRADUATE

Be prepared to...
....

Always keep..

....

Focus on..

never..

Always remember...

....

Be open to..

Surround yourself with..

I wish you...

....

(one last thing)..

BEST WISHES ∘∘∘∘∘∘∘∘∘∘∘∘∘∘∘∘∘∘∘∘∘∘∘∘∘∘∘∘∘∘∘∘∘∘∘

ADVICE AND WISHES FOR THE GRADUATE

Be prepared to...
....

Always keep..
....

Focus on..

never..

Always remember..
....

Be open to...

Surround yourself with...

I wish you..
....

(one last thing)..

BEST WISHES ○○○○○○○○○○○○○○○○○○○○○○○○○○○○○○○○

ADVICE AND WISHES FOR THE GRADUATE

Be prepared to...

....

Always keep...

....

Focus on...

never...

Always remember..

....

Be open to...

Surround yourself with..

I wish you...

....

(one last thing)..

BEST WISHES ·····························

ADVICE AND WISHES FOR THE GRADUATE

Be prepared to..

....

Always keep...

....

Focus on..

never..

Always remember...

....

Be open to..

Surround yourself with..

I wish you..

....

(one last thing)..

BEST WISHES ∘∘∘∘∘∘∘∘∘∘∘∘∘∘∘∘∘∘∘∘∘∘∘∘∘∘∘∘∘∘∘∘∘∘∘∘∘

ADVICE AND WISHES FOR THE GRADUATE

Be prepared to...

....

Always keep...

....

Focus on...

never...

Always remember...

....

Be open to...

Surround yourself with...

I wish you...

....

(one last thing)...

BEST WISHES °°°°°°°°°°°°°°°°°°°°°°°°°°°°°°°°°°°°°°

ADVICE AND WISHES FOR THE GRADUATE

Be prepared to...
....
Always keep..
....
Focus on..
never...
Always remember..
....
Be open to..
Surround yourself with..
I wish you..
....
(one last thing)..

BEST WISHES °°

ADVICE AND WISHES FOR THE GRADUATE

Be prepared to...

....

Always keep...

....

Focus on..

never...

Always remember..

....

Be open to..

Surround yourself with...

I wish you..

....

(one last thing)..

BEST WISHES ....

ADVICE AND WISHES FOR THE GRADUATE

Be prepared to..

....

Always keep..

....

Focus on...

never..

Always remember..

....

Be open to..

Surround yourself with..

I wish you...

....

(one last thing)..

BEST WISHES ....

ADVICE AND WISHES FOR THE GRADUATE

Be prepared to..
....
Always keep..
....
Focus on..
never...
Always remember..
....
Be open to..
Surround yourself with..
I wish you..
....
(one last thing)...

BEST WISHES ○○○○○○○○○○○○○○○○○○○○○○○○○○○○○○○○○○○○

ADVICE AND WISHES FOR THE GRADUATE

Be prepared to..

....

Always keep..

....

Focus on...

never..

Always remember..

....

Be open to...

Surround yourself with...

I wish you...

....

(one last thing)...

BEST WISHES ∘∘∘∘∘∘∘∘∘∘∘∘∘∘∘∘∘∘∘∘∘∘∘∘∘∘∘∘∘∘∘∘∘∘∘∘∘∘

ADVICE AND WISHES FOR THE GRADUATE

Be prepared to...
....

Always keep..
....

Focus on...

never..

Always remember...
....

Be open to...

Surround yourself with..

I wish you...
....

(one last thing)...

BEST WISHES ∘∘∘∘∘∘∘∘∘∘∘∘∘∘∘∘∘∘∘∘∘∘∘∘∘∘∘∘∘∘∘∘∘∘∘∘∘∘∘

ADVICE AND WISHES FOR THE GRADUATE

Be prepared to...

....

Always keep...

....

Focus on...

never...

Always remember...

....

Be open to...

Surround yourself with...

I wish you...

....

(one last thing)..

BEST WISHES ∘∘∘∘∘∘∘∘∘∘∘∘∘∘∘∘∘∘∘∘∘∘∘∘∘∘∘∘∘∘∘∘∘∘∘

ADVICE AND WISHES FOR THE GRADUATE

Be prepared to...

....

Always keep...

....

Focus on..

never..

Always remember..

....

Be open to...

Surround yourself with...

I wish you..

....

(one last thing)...

BEST WISHES ∘∘∘∘∘∘∘∘∘∘∘∘∘∘∘∘∘∘∘∘∘∘∘∘∘∘∘∘∘∘∘∘∘

ADVICE AND WISHES FOR THE GRADUATE

Be prepared to...

....

Always keep..

....

Focus on..

never..

Always remember...

....

Be open to...

Surround yourself with..

I wish you...

....

(one last thing)..

BEST WISHES °°°

ADVICE AND WISHES FOR THE GRADUATE

Be prepared to..

....

Always keep..

....

Focus on..

never..

Always remember..

....

Be open to..

Surround yourself with..

I wish you..

....

(one last thing)..

BEST WISHES ∘∘∘

Made in United States
Cleveland, OH
22 May 2025

17136224R00057